A DISPLAY of GOD'S GLORY

THIRD EDITION

(888) 543-1030
525 A Street, NE
Washington, DC 20002
www.9marks.org

ISBN 0-9701252-2-4

All Scripture quotations from
The New International Version.

A DISPLAY of GOD'S GLORY

BASICS OF CHURCH STRUCTURE
Deacons, Elders, Congregationalism & Membership

Mark Dever

One of the most important issues facing local churches today is leadership. Even though books abound that deal with the character and effectiveness of leaders, much confusion still exists regarding the roles, responsibilities and authority of pastors and lay leaders, particularly with reference to the organization and governance of the church. Dr. Dever's work is a must read for any pastor or lay leader who is seeking to lead healthy and effective churches. He provides great clarity and insight both to the theological and practical aspects of the issues related to elders, deacons, pastors, lay leaders, and membership, all within the context of historic congregational church governance. Dr. Dever provides the most succinct and clear treatment that I have read related to organizing and leading a biblically healthy and effective church.

—*Brad Waggoner, Ph.D.*
Vice President of the B&H Publishing Group

A Display of God's Glory speaks biblically to an area in which and at a time when there is great need for reform in our churches. The strength of this booklet lies principally in its commitment to the sufficiency of Scripture, specifically at this point where there is so much pragmatism afoot. Dever's unflinching announcement of the Bible as both his starting point and his constant guide should invite both our trust and our self-examination. *Display* is marked by a practical wisdom that flows from a glad-hearted commitment to Scripture's sufficiency but also from an equally glad-hearted trust in the wisdom and goodness of God as seen in the biblical design of the church. There is, at present, an insufficient number of treatments of this subject from a thoroughly and thoughtfully biblical standpoint. Here is one-made all the more useful by its condensed, focused approach.

—*Mike Bullmore*
Senior Pastor of CrossWay Community Church,
Kenosha, Wisconsin

A succinct and helpful guidebook showing how one congregation of believers has organized its corporate life under Christ. Mark Dever draws on biblical principles refracted through the wisdom of the Baptist heritage and lived out in the midst of a growing, dynamic congregation in the heart of our nation's capital. Not everyone will agree with every detail in this book, but no one who takes the New Testament seriously can ignore the questions posed here.

—Timothy George
Dean of Beeson Divinity School, Samford University

The greatest virtues of this booklet are Dever's able marshalling of all the biblical evidence and the translating of it into an approach to church structure that answers the nuts and bolts questions of implementation. Each chapter points the way to healthy church polity—biblical deacon ministry, plurality of elders within an overall congregationalism, and a case for the importance of church membership. To those who have felt that something is wrong with our church structure, this booklet points the way to a biblical, God-glorifying approach.

— John Hammett
Professor of Theology
Southeastern Baptist Theological Seminary

Mark Dever's work is like a gearshift for church leaders seeking to accelerate real reformation in their churches. It provides clear and Biblical answers to the many questions pastors and laymen alike have about these important issues. I wish it had been available to me in the early years of my pastoral ministry. I'll be recommending this tool in my seminary classes and all over the country.

—Don Whitney
Assistant Professor of Spiritual Formation
Southern Baptist Theological Seminary

*To Capitol Hill Baptist Church,
the congregation that God, in His
loving grace, has called me to
know, serve, and love.*

TABLE OF CONTENTS

INTRODUCTION

How do you see the invisible God? By looking at the local Christian congregation.

How do we come to that answer? Follow me for a minute. When our first parents in the Garden of Eden sinned, human beings lost sight of God. He placed us under his curse. We became exiles.

Since then, a few people have been given some kind of partial vision of God, such as Moses' limited look (Ex. 33:18-23; Heb. 11:27). And there are a few other such examples.

Then came Christ. Jesus told Thomas, "Anyone who has seen me has seen the Father" (John 14:9). Jesus "is the image of the invisible God" (Col. 1:15). Jesus is the clearest picture of the invisible God to us in this world. But Jesus is no longer visible, at least not in the sense that you and I are. He is not open to inspection by the physical eye. And yet, one of the most common images for the local church is that of "the body of Christ." It is in the church that God's Spirit—the Spirit of Jesus—rules and reigns, and is made visible in the lives of love that we live. As Paul said to the Ephesians, a grand portrayal of God's wisdom is being presented in the church. God's "intent was that now, through the church, the manifold wisdom of God should be made known . . . " (Eph. 3:10).

And this is not simply God's plan for one future day when the vast assembly of the redeemed will be gathered before God's throne. God intends to display His glory through the local church today, as Christians live together in patience, forgiveness, justice, mercy and love. We reflect God's own character by the character of our congregation's life. Therefore, every aspect of the church's life is worth our careful consideration. Even of it's polity!

I remember using the word "polity" in a paper I wrote in the 8th grade and having the word circled by my 24-year old English teacher as an error. It was with juvenile glee that I took the dictionary to her, opened it, and read to her something like "the organization created for managing affairs, especially public affairs; government." (Can you imagine how a kid like me fit in!) Polity, then, is management, organization, government, and structures of authority.

As Christians, we strive to establish our lives on the teaching of Scripture. The question must be asked, therefore, does Scripture deal clearly with questions about the polity, or organization, of the church? If so, what does Scripture teach? Of course, we Christians believe that Scripture is sufficient for our preaching and discipling, for our spirituality and joy in following Christ, for church growth and our understanding of evangelism. But is Scripture even *meant* to tell us how we are to organize our lives together as Christians in our churches, or are we left simply to find our own best practices? Is our church polity a matter indifferent? Is it a matter to be determined on the basis of mere pragmatism, by whatever seems to work best and avoid problems?

I believe that God has revealed in His Word all that we need to know in order to love and serve Him, and this includes what we need to know even about organizing our churches. This sufficiency of Scripture for the corporate lives of our churches has been assumed in the confessions of Baptists, Congregationalists, Presbyterians, and many others in years past, and it has been assumed by those men whom God has called to fill our pulpits. Let me be clear. When we say that church polity can be found in the pages of the New Testament, that does not mean that we assume our own practices are correct and then go in search of ways to justify them biblically. Rather, our goal must be to look at the Bible, recognize some basic aspects of structure and organization that it teaches, and then organize our churches accordingly. The pages of the New Testament are filled with examples of how the early Christians structured their churches. In its pages we find that there were clear corporate meetings (Acts 20:7; Heb. 10:25), elections (Acts 1:23-26; 6:5-6), officers (e.g., Phil. 1:1; Acts 20:17, 28), instances of discipline (I Cor. 5), contributions (Rom. 15:26; I Cor. 16:1-2), letters of commendation (Acts 18:27; II Cor. 3:1), the administration of the ordinances (Acts 2:41; I Cor. 11:23-26), and qualifications for membership (Matt. 28:19; Acts 2:47). Clearly, God has given us in His Word direction about many aspects of the church's corporate life and structure.

It is wonderful for us that He does so! Being certain that God's Word is meant to regulate our lives together, even in the organization of our churches, frees us from the tyranny of the latest fashion. Some pastors today may feel that we *must* have choirs and committees, but that we *may* have sermons (if we don't feel that a video ministry is ready yet to fill that time slot); or that we *may* have membership (if we can't think of anything more creative to do). God's Word, though, realigns our thinking on the church: We find that the Bible lays out clear parameters for our instruction (though within those parameters there is flexibility). We begin to learn that we *must* have preaching and membership, and that we *may* have choirs and committees.

Pastor John L. Dagg (1794-1884) wrote that

Church order and the ceremonials of religion, are less important than a new heart; and in the view of some, any laborious investigation of questions respecting them may appear to be needless and unprofitable. But we know, from the Holy Scriptures, that Christ gave commands on these subjects, and we cannot refuse to obey. Love prompts our obedience; and love prompts also the search which may be necessary to ascertain his will. Let us, therefore, prosecute the investigations which are before us, with a fervent prayer, that the Holy Spirit, who guides into all truth, may assist us to learn the will of him whom we supremely love and adore. (Manual of Church Order, p. 12)

Recognizing this, we do well to consider Scripture's teaching about a few central aspects of the church's polity. So many questions could be considered, but I want to focus on what Scripture teaches on four of the most basic components of church polity—deacons, elders, congregationalism, and membership. May God use our efforts to help us better understand His intentions for our life together in the church.

What's been updated for this third edition? The changes to the text have been slight. No changes in the basic ideas of the book have been made. Reformatting for ease of reading made repagination necessary, and therefore we took the opportunity to make a few small improvements.

6

DEACONS

I. **"Deacon" Defined**
   A. Service in the New Testament World
   B. Service in the Bible
   C. Maintaining a Distinction between Deacons
      and Elders

II. **Historical Background**
   A. The Early Church
   B. Duties of Early Church Deacons
   C. The Roman and Greek Churches
   D. The Lutheran Church
   E. Deacons in the Reformation
   F. The Presbyterian Church
   G. Baptist and Congregational Churches

III. **The Three Purposes of Deacons in Acts 6**
   A. To Meet Physical Needs
   B. To Promote Unity of the Body
      1. The Goal of all Spiritual Gifts
      2. No Small-mindedness in Deacons
   C. To Support the Ministry of the Word
      1. Deacons are not a Second House of the
         Legislature
      2. Deacons Coordinate Particular Ministries

IV. **Qualifications of Deacons**
   A. I Timothy 3
   B. Women as Deacons

V. **Summary**

Chapter I

DEACONS

Let's begin with one of the most familiar offices in local churches today—the office of deacon. Depending on what kind of church you come from, "deacon" may conjure up images of gray-haired bankers sitting around long, highly-varnished tables in opulently appointed church parlors. Or the word could bring to mind earnest servants of the church coordinating needs-based ministries, evangelistic outreach, or pastoral care. This is what deacons are in our churches. What are they in the Bible?

I. "Deacon" Defined

The New Testament world was similar to our own in the way it viewed servanthood. Service to others was not admired by the Greeks. Instead, they primarily admired the development of one's own character and personality, always with an eye to maintaining self-respect. Diaconal service to others was seen as what we would describe by the pejorative term "servile." *Service in the New Testament World*

The Bible, though, presents service quite differently. In our modern translations of the New Testament, the word diakonos is usually translated as "servant," but sometimes as "minister," and sometimes it is just transliterated as "deacon." It can refer to service in general (e.g., Acts 1:17, 25; 19:22; Rom. 12:7; I Cor. 12:5; 16:15; Eph. 4:12; Col. 4:17; II Tim. 1:18; Philemon 13; Heb. 6:10; I Pet 4:10-11; Rev. 2:19), to rulers in particu- *Service in the Bible* lar (e.g., Rom. 13:4), or to caring for physical needs (e.g., Matt. 25:44; Acts 11:29; 12:25; Rom. 15:25, 31; II Cor. 8:4, 19-20; 9:1, 12-13; 11:8). It is clear in the New Testament that women can do at least some of this serving (e.g., Matt. 8:15; Mark 1:31; Luke 4:39; Matt. 27:55; Mark 15:41; cf. Luke 8:3; Luke 10:40; John 12:2; Rom. 16:1). Angels serve in this way (e.g., Matt. 4:11; Mark 1:13). It sometimes refers specifically to waiting tables (e.g., Matt. 22:13; Luke 10:40; 17:8; John 2:5, 9; 12:2), and though such service was despised in the Greek world, Jesus regarded it very differently. In John 12:26 Jesus said, "Whoever deacons me must follow me; and where I am, my deacon also will be. My Father will honor the one who deacons me." Again in Matt. 20:26 (cf. Mark 9:35) Jesus said, "whoever wants to be great, must be your deacon." And in Matt. 23:11 (cf. Mark 10:43; Luke 22:26-27) he said that "the greatest among you will be your deacon."

In fact, Jesus even presented himself as a type of deacon (e.g., Matt. 20:28; Mark 10:45; Luke 22:26-27; cf. John 13; Luke 12:37; Romans 15:8). Christians are presented as being deacons of Christ or His Gospel. That's how the apostles are depicted (Acts 6:1-7), and it is certainly how Paul regularly refers to himself and to those who worked with him (e.g., Acts 20:24: I Cor. 3:5; II Cor. 3:3, 6-9; 4:1; 5:18; 6:3-4; 11:23; Eph. 3:7; Col. 1:23; I Tim. 1:12; II Tim. 4:11). He referred to himself as a deacon among the Gentiles, the particular group he was called specially to serve (Acts 21:19; Rom. 11:13). Paul calls Timothy a deacon of Christ (e.g., I Tim. 4:6; II Tim. 4:5), and Peter says that the Old Testament prophets were deacons to us Christians (I Pet. 1:12). Angels are called deacons (Heb. 1:14), and even Satan, too, has his deacons (II Cor. 3:6-9; 11:15; Gal. 2:17).

Maintaining a Distinction Between Deacons and Elders

We should always be careful to maintain a distinction between the ministry of deacons and the ministry of elders. In one sense both elders and deacons are involved in "deaconing," but that service takes on two very different forms. It is in the first seven verses of Acts 6 that we find the crucial passage where deaconing is divided between traditional deaconing (table-waiting, physical service), and the kind of "deaconing" of the Word to which the apostles (and later, elders) were called. The deacons described in Acts 6 are very much like the church's waiters, at least in an administrative sense. They are to care for the physical needs of the church. Establishing a group with this particular ministry is important because a failure to do so can result in these two types of deaconing—of the Word (elders) and of tables (deacons)—being confused with one another and one of them thus being forgotten. Churches should neglect neither the preaching of the Word, nor the practical care for the members that helps to foster unity and that fills out our duties to love one another. Both of these aspects of a church's life and ministry are important. In order to assure that we have both kinds of deaconing going on in our churches, we should distinguish the ministries of the deacons from those of the elders.

II. Historical Background

During the time of the apostles, the situation in churches was fairly fluid, though a plurality of elders and a plurality of deacons seem fairly constant. Immediately after New Testament times, these separate offices of elders and deacons continued. The role of elders began to be distinguished between bishops and priests, but deacons continued being always listed with and after the bishops and priests, usually being seen as those who were tasked fundamentally with assisting the bishops or overseers. In the early church, the office generally seems to have been held for life. The functions of the office, however, varied from place to place. Diaconal duties might include:

The Early Church

- reading or singing Scripture in church;
- receiving the offerings and keeping records of who gave;
- distributing the offerings to the bishops, presbyters, and themselves, to the unmarried women and widows, and to the poor;
- distributing communion;
- leading prayers during services, and giving a signal for those who were not to take communion to leave before the ordinance was administered.

This would be a pretty good summary of the duties of deacons from the 2nd through the 6th centuries.

As the monarchical episcopate developed, so did a kind of monarchical diaconate beneath it. As the role of bishop developed, so did the role of archdeacon. The archdeacon was the chief deacon of a particular place, and might be described as a deputy concerned with material matters. It is not surprising to note that the archdeacon in Rome became particularly important. Suffice it to say that abuses crept in and that deacons, and especially archdeacons, became quite wealthy. How ironic that those who were meant to serve others instead used others to serve their own desires! For a number of reasons, the deacons' influence declined in the middle ages. Caring for the poor became more a vehicle for the contributors to gain credit with God in order to, as they conceived it, lessen their time in purgatory.

The Eastern Orthodox church has always kept separate deacons—laymen who served in that capacity. In the west, though, by the late Middle Ages being a deacon had become merely a step on the way to being ordained as a priest, that is, an elder. Deacons in the Roman Catholic and the Episcopalian churches are still just that—trainee ministers who serve as deacons for one year before becoming full-fledged priests. The

Second Vatican Council has re-opened the possibility of a different, permanent, more biblical kind of deacon in the Roman Catholic Church.

Luther recovered the church's responsibility to care physically for the church and especially for the poor in the church, though Lutheran churches didn't recover the idea of the New Testament deacon. In the Lutheran churches today, practice varies. In some places deacons are unordained, but in other places any ordained assistant minister would be called a deacon, particularly those with responsibilities for pastoral care and evangelism. — The Lutheran Church

In many of the more evangelical Protestant churches during the Reformation, the biblical practice of having deacons distinct from elders or pastors was recognized. At the time of the Reformation, some Protestants, like Martin Butzer at Cambridge, urged that the duties of the deacons should be re-established. In each church, they said, the deacons should distinguish between the deserving and the undeserving poor, discretely investigating and quietly caring for the needs of the one and expelling the other from the church. They should also keep written records, as they were able, of funds given by church members. — Deacons in the Reformation

In the Presbyterian church, deacons are those who administer the alms and care for the poor and sick (though we might argue that these functions have largely been taken over by the secular state). The deacons are a separate body from the elders and are responsible to them. This is how many Baptist and Congregational churches were once organized. Some still are organized in this way, and most have at least to some degree maintained this structure. — The Presbyterian Church

In many Baptist and Congregational churches, however, more definitely spiritual functions are assigned to the deacons. They assist the pastor in various ways, especially in distributing the elements at the Lord's — Baptist and Congregational Churches

Supper, and have evolved into a kind of executive and financial board for the church, particularly in congregations that no longer have boards of elders. Deacons often serve actively for limited periods of time, though the recognition of a person as a deacon is usually considered permanent.

That's how Christians have done it. Now, do the Scriptures have any word for us by which to reform our practices?

III. The Three Purposes of Deacons in Acts 6

As we have seen, the *diakonos* words appear many times in the New Testament. The clearest picture, though, comes perhaps from Acts 6, where we think the first deacons were set aside. From that account, we may note three aspects of the deacons' ministry among us.

To Meet Physical Needs

First, deacons are to care for the physical needs of the church. Read Acts 6:1. Some of the Christians "were being overlooked in the daily distribution of food." We have noted that the root of the word deacon means minister or servant, and particularly was used of table-waiters at the time, or of various types of service, usually either physical or financial. In Acts 6:2, the Apostles characterized this service as *"waiting on tables,"* or literally *"deaconing tables."* This is the first aspect of deacon ministry – meeting physical needs. It is important to note that the deacons in Acts 6 likely didn't do all the deaconing themselves; rather these few deacons probably organized many other Christians in the church to ensure that the work would be done.

Caring for people, especially for other Christians – and most especially for other members of our own congregation – is important for three reasons: for the physical well-being of those concerned; for their spiritual well-being; and as a witness to those outside.

What did Jesus say in John 13? "This is how the world will know that you are my disciples, by the love you have for one another." The physical care presented in this passage demonstrates just that kind of Christ-like love.

Behind this, though, we see that there is a purpose not just for those in need, but for the body as a whole. **This is the second aspect of the kind of deacon ministry we see in Acts 6—it is centered on the unity of the body.**

If you look at this passage in a more abstract way, you could ask, "In caring for these widows, what were they really doing?" They were working to make the food distribution among the widows more equitable. That's true, but why was that important? Because this *physical* neglect was causing a *spiritual* disunity in the body. That's how the passage begins in 6:1, "In those days, when the number of disciples was increasing, the Grecian Jews among them complained against those of the Aramaic-speaking community because their widows were being overlooked in the daily distribution of food." One group of Christians was beginning to complain against another group. This seems to be what arrested the attention of the Apostles. They were not merely trying to rectify a problem in the benevolence ministry of the church. They were trying to stop the church's unity from fracturing, and that in a particularly dangerous way: along traditional cultural lines of division. The deacons were appointed to head off disunity in the church.

Really, this is the goal for all the gifts that God's Spirit gives to His church—to build one another up and encourage each other (e.g., Rom. 1:11-12). Paul says to the Corinthians that God's gifts are "for the common good" (I Cor. 12:4-7, 12). He exhorts these early Christians, "Since you are eager to have spiritual gifts, try to excel in gifts that build up the church" (I Cor.

To Promote Unity of the Body

The Goal of Spiritual Gifts

12:12). So Paul says in I Cor. 14:26, "all must be done for strengthening." As John Calvin said, commenting on I Cor. 14:12, "The more anxious a person is to devote himself to upbuilding, the more highly Paul wishes him to be regarded." So Peter wrote, "Each should use whatever gift he has received to serve others administering God's grace" (I Pet. 4:10).

No Small-mindedness in Deacons

Edifying and uniting the church is especially the ministry of the deacons as we see it in Acts 6. Therefore, we cannot have people serve us well as deacons who are unhappy with the church. The deacons are not those in the church who are complaining the loudest or jarring the church with their actions or attitudes. Quite the opposite! The deacons are to be the mufflers, the shock-absorbers.

Therefore, among those who would serve a church as a deacon there must be no small-mindedness. Such members must not be given to "turfiness"—caring about their area, their rights and prerogatives in that area, or even quietly resenting service by others who would interlope into their sphere! Deacons are not set apart to advocate their cause, or argue for their corners like representatives or lobbyists. Instead, they are to come on behalf of the whole—to serve particular needs, yes—but with a sense of the whole, a sense that their work contributes to the health of the whole. Even more, they are to be able to help others come to understand this particular ministry as a part of the uniting and edifying of the church as a whole. They are to be builders of the church by being servants who help to bind us together with cords of kindness and of loving service.

Support of the Ministry of the Word

Thirdly, these men were appointed to support the ministry of the Word. In Acts 6:3, the Apostles seem to acknowledge that caring for physical needs was a responsibility that the church, and therefore in some sense they themselves, had. But they said in 6:3 that they would turn this responsibility over to another group within the church. In that sense, these deacons were not only helping the body as a whole, but in so doing, they were helping to support these apostles/ elders, whose main obligations lay elsewhere.

So the deacons were not a separate power block in the church. They were not a second house of the legislature, through which bills needed to be passed. They were *servants* who served the church as a whole by helping with the responsibilities that the main teachers could not perform. Deacons supported the teachers of the Word in their ministry. They were fundamentally encouragers and supporters of the ministry of the elders. If this is the case, then it is the most supportive people in the church who should serve the church as the deacons. We should look for gifts of encouragement, so that more, not fewer, people will be blessed by their service.

Deacons Are Not a Second House of the Legislature

At our church in Washington, D.C., we recognize our deacons not as a deliberative body, but rather as those people in our church who coordinate particular needed ministries in the church. What we hope and pray is that each one of those who serve as deacons will help to unify us through various ministries, helping individuals, helping the body, and glorifying God in it all. We have a deacon who supervises our ministry of hospitality, another who coordinates our ministry through the radio and website, another who handles our sound system, and another for member care. At this writing we have fourteen different deacons serving us in diaconal positions. We regularly retire positions that no longer seem to need coordination, and split burgeoning ones into two, or even create new ones as needs and opportunities in the body become apparent to us.

Deacons Coordinate Particular Ministries

We hope that these deacons will be some of the leading utilizers of the church's human resources. We hope that they will be diligent in praying for us, in getting to know the whole body, in seeing how the services that they coordinate can forward the ministry of the church as a whole. We recognize that this service that they perform for us is costly. They must understand their deaconship as their main ministry in the church while they serve in that position. But what a blessing such servants are to us as they develop hearts of service in other brothers and sisters, training them to see the role of this or that particular ministry in building up the church! Through their activity and creativity, our deacons will bless our church for far longer than they hold the office.

IV. Qualifications of Deacons

I Timothy 3

In I Timothy 3:8-13, Paul spells out to Timothy, the pastor of the church in Ephesus, what these deacons should be like. Combining the characteristics listed there with the qualities of those selected in Acts 6, we can certainly say that those who serve us as deacons should be known to be full of the Holy Spirit (because though concerned with physical things, theirs is certainly a spiritual ministry). These deacons should be known to be full of wisdom. They should be chosen by the congregation, with the congregation's confidence. They should willingly and diligently take on the responsibility for the particular needs their ministry is meant to serve. They should be worthy of respect, sincere, not indulging in much wine, not pursuing dishonest gain, keeping hold of the deep truths of the faith with a clear conscience, tested and approved servants who are the husband of but one wife and who manage their own children and household well.

Women as Deacons

That deacons are commanded to be the "husband of one wife" does not preclude the service of women in diaconal positions. The example of Phoebe in Romans 16:1, the use of "deacon" words elsewhere of women in the Scriptures, and to a lesser degree, the long history of deaconnesses in Baptist churches, has led our own church happily to embrace the ministry of women serving us as deacons. Yet because of I Timothy 2 and of the larger Biblical picture of male headship, we would discourage churches from recognizing women as deacons if their office were confused with that of the elders (as deacons are in so many churches today). It is our clarity about the distinct role of elders, and the fact that those elders must be males, that enables us to encourage freely the service of our sisters as deacons or deaconesses recognized by the church.

V. Summary

In summary, the New Testament would seem to bring together the three aspects of deacon ministry that we've noted in Acts 6—care for physical needs to the end of uniting the Body under the ministers of the Word. Deacons are to support the ministry of the elders, unite the Body, and care for the needy. They are to be encouragers, peace-makers and servants. As Dietrich Bonhoeffer said, "The church does not need brilliant personalities but faithful servants of Jesus and the brethren," (Bonhoeffer, *Life Together,* p. 109).

ELDERS

I.   **Plurality of Elders**

II. **Qualifications for Elders**
     A. Women are not to be Elders
     B. I Timothy 3
     C. The Point of Leadership in the Church
     D. Finding Godly Leaders in our Churches

III. **Historical Overview**
     A. Original words for "Elder"
     B. Presbyterians and Elders
     C. Baptists and Elders

IV. **Relationship of Elders and Church Staff**

V.   **Relationship of Elders and Deacons**
     A. Similarities in Qualifications
     B. Root of the Distinction—Acts 6
     C. Teaching and Authority

VI. **Relationship of the Elders and "The" Pastor**
     A. "Pastor" in the New Testament
     B. Glimpses of the Pastoral Role
        1. Some men moved from place to place
        2. Some were supported full-time by the church
        3. Paul wrote particularly to Timothy
        4. Jesus wrote to "the messenger of the church"
     C. The Pastor as Elder

VI. **Relationship of the Elders and the Church**
     A. Five Characteristics
        1. Clear recognition
        2. Heart-felt trust
        3. Evident godliness
        4. Sincere carefulness
        5. Beneficial results
     B. Regard for Pastors

VIII. **On the Gift of Authority**

Chapter II

ELDERS

As important as the deacons are, even more fundamental to our life together as Christians is the ministry
of another group, to which we now turn—the elders.

I. Plurality of elders

The first thing we should note about the elders of a
local church is that they are elders plural. Though a
specific number of elders for a particular congregation
is never mentioned, the New Testament regularly
refers to "elders" in the plural (e.g., Acts 16:4; 20:17;
21:18; Titus 1:5; James 5:14). The elders of Israel that
we see referred to throughout the Gospels and Acts are
plural. The elders in Heaven are plural (Rev. 5:14;
11:16; 19:4). In Acts 11:30, elders are plural. In Acts
14:21-23 we read, "They preached the good news in
that city (Derbe) and won a large number of disciples.
Then they returned to Lystra, Iconium, and Antioch,
strengthening the disciples and encouraging them to
remain true to the faith.... Paul and Barnabas appointed [or had elected] elders for them in each church and,
with prayer and fasting, committed them to the Lord
in whom they had put their trust." If you look through
Acts 15, you find in verses 2, 4, 6, 22 and 23 that there
are plural elders. In Acts 16:4, the word for elder occurs
in the plural. In Acts 20:17, we read that Paul called to
himself the elders of the church in Ephesus. So too, in
Acts 21:28, and in I Timothy 4:14 and 5:17. In Titus 1:5,

Paul says, "The reason I left you in Crete was that you might straighten out what was left unfinished and appoint elders in every town.... " James in James 5:14 envisions the elders (plural) of the local church (singular) coming to pray with one who is sick. In I Peter 5:1, Peter appeals to the elders among these Christians. In fact, the only exceptions are in II and III John, where the writer simply refers to himself as "the elder," and in I Timothy 5, where there is a bit of church case law about what we should do if there is an accusation against an elder. But basically, the picture in the New Testament is that there is normally within the local church a body of elders, not simply one elder.

II. Qualifications for Elders

Women are not to be Elders

Who should be an elder? What should their qualifications be? The qualifications for an elder are laid out clearly in the Bible in I Timothy 3 and in Titus 1.

Before we turn to I Timothy 3, though, we need to take note of an important issue raised in I Timothy 2—that it is not God's will for women to serve as elders. While many questions have been raised about an obscure phrase in I Timothy 2, it is always safer to begin with the clear parts of Scripture and pray that God will shed light on the more obscure parts, rather than doubting the clear parts because of the presence of obscure parts. What is clear in I Timothy 2 is that a woman should not teach or have authority over a man. Whatever the exact authority Paul intended to speak of here as inappropriate, it clearly involves the woman teaching. The practice of the early church was to have the creation order of the authority of the husband over the wife reflected in the practice of the church. Galatians 3:28 is clear that in Christ there is neither male nor female, but this is meant not to eliminate all distinctions between the genders, but rather is simply an affirmation of the wonderfully impartial grace of God in salvation.

Given that, let's look at the list in I Timothy 3. Take a I Timothy 3
few minutes to read I Timothy 3:1-7. D.A. Carson (professor of New Testament at Trinity Evangelical Divinity
School) noted once that this list of characteristics is
most notable for being not very notable at all. What he
meant is that all of these characteristics are elsewhere
in the Bible enjoined on all Christians—all of them,
that is, except for the ability to teach (I Tim. 3:2). While
the Scriptures are sufficient to teach us here about the
character of an elder, I do not think that Paul would
claim that this particular list is exhaustive. Rather, his
purpose was to list characteristics which would generally have been recognized as virtuous even by the sur-
rounding culture of the time.

The point of leadership in the church is to bring The Point of
glory to God by commending the truth to outsiders. Leadership in the Church
This is why Paul was so incensed at the Corinthians for
going to secular court against each other and for
allowing those living flagrantly ungodly lives to be
associated with the church. Both of these things would
undermine the witness of the gospel. So in Paul's first
letter to Timothy, the evident ungodliness of some of
the false teachers in the Ephesian church was jeopar-
dizing the whole way that God would be glorified
through the church—the proclamation of the gospel of
forgiveness and hope, and the conversion of sinners!
The list of virtues which Paul gave in I Timothy 3 (or
Titus 1, for that matter) are not all of the virtues which
a Christian should exhibit. They are virtues which
would have commended the gospel to those who were
watching the church's leaders. Regular Bible reading is
good, and prayer is necessary, but Paul mentions neither here. Nevertheless, I want both of these virtues in
my elders! I am taught elsewhere in the Bible that they
are to characterize all Christians, but I think for Paul's
purposes here, he wanted to emphasize things like
paying bills on time, being cheerful, humble and helpful—things that even most pagans recognize as good.

Finding Godly
Leaders
in Our
Churches

How do we find such leaders in our churches? We pray for God's wisdom. We study His Word, particularly those passages in I Timothy and Titus that teach clearly about the qualifications for such responsibility. We should not follow the world's standards in picking our leaders. We should not imitate those churches that simply find the community leaders in the congregation, and then make them the leaders in the church. Os Guiness in his book *Dining with the Devil* recounts the comment of a Japanese businessman to a visiting Australian: "Whenever I meet a Buddhist leader, I meet a holy man. Whenever I meet a Christian leader, I meet a manager" (p.49). Instead of this, we are to search for those men of the character, reputation, ability to handle the Word, and fruitfulness which marks a good leader in the church. The character of these church leaders is to be built not for themselves, but for others. Thus, they are not to be lovers of money, but lovers of strangers—that's what "hospitable" literally means. True church leaders will be other-centered.

III. Historical Overview

Original Words
for "Elder"

All churches have had individuals who performed the functions of elders, even if they called them by other names. The two most common New Testament names for this office were *episcopos* (overseer) and *presbuteros* (elder).

Presbyterians
and Elders

When evangelicals today hear the word "elder," many immediately think "Presbyterian." However, the first Congregationalists back in the sixteenth century taught that eldership was an office in a New Testament church. While it is historically accurate to associate elders with Presbyterians, it is *not* accurate to associate them *exclusively* with Presbyterians; nor is it true to think that the term is foreign to Baptists.

Baptists
and Elders

Elders could be found in Baptist churches in America throughout the 18th century and into the

19th century, (e.g., A. T. Robertson, *Life of Broadus*, p. 34; O. L. Hailey, *J. R. Graves*, p. 40). W. B. Johnson, the first president of the Southern Baptist Convention, wrote a book on church life in which he strongly advocated the idea of a plurality of elders in one local church. Whether through inattention to Scripture, or the pressure of life on the frontier (where churches were springing up at an amazing rate!), the practice of cultivating such textured leadership declined. But Baptist papers' discussion of reviving this biblical office continued. As late as the early twentieth century, Baptist publications were referring to leaders by the title of "elder." Though this practice is unusual among Baptist churches today, there is now a growing trend back to it—and for good reason. It was needed in New Testament churches, and it is needed now.

Let me help define for you what we mean by elder here by distinguishing the elders first from the church staff, then from the deacons, and then by asking about the relationship of the pastor to the other elders.

IV. Relationship of Elders and Church Staff

Many modern churches have tended to confuse elders with the church staff. The staff are the people that the church has set aside full-time to work for the church. They are often the people most directly familiar with what is going on day to day. They often have seminary training. They must have a certain degree of godliness and maturity or they would never have been hired in the first place. Certainly members of the church staff may be elders. In fact, our church's constitution requires us to call no one as the pastor here who we would not also immediately recognize as an elder. That, I think, is a wise provision. However, our constitution also requires that the majority of our elders *not* be in the pay of the church. For example, our pastoral assistants (young men, useful in ministry, likely heading off to seminary soon) are not generally recognized as elders, though they provide wonderful care for us in everything from teaching to visiting. The reason we included this provision in our constitution is precisely because we desire to make sure that we as a congregation feel the weight of the responsibility not simply to hire elders, but to try to be the kind of spiritually fruitful church that sees them raised up among us. Of the five elders currently recognized in our church, three have secular jobs and only two, myself as pastor and our church administrator, are in the paid employ of the church.

V. Relationship of Elders and Deacons

In practice, if not in doctrine, many churches have confused the New Testament roles of deacon and elder. The concerns of the deacons, as we have seen, are the practical details of church life: administration, maintenance, and the care of church members with physical needs—all in order to promote the unity of the church and the ministry of the Word.

Similarities in Qualifications

In I Timothy 3, what is most noticeable in comparing the lists of qualifications for elder and then for deacons is not their differences, but their similarities. Both overseers (elders) and deacons need to be reputable, blameless, trusted, monogamous, sober, temperate, generous individuals. Indeed, so similar are these two lists of traits, that the striking thing is that with such similar qualifications, Paul and these early Christians should so clearly recognize *two separate bodies of leaders.*

The Root of the Distinction

In Acts 6, we have seen something of the root of the distinction in the roles and responsibilities of the deacons and the elders. In Acts 6:2, after the complaining in the church at Jerusalem had begun, we read, "So the Twelve gathered all the disciples together and said, 'It would not be right for us to neglect the ministry of the

Word of God in order to wait on tables.'" From this, we could say that the ministry of the Word of God is central to the responsibility of the elders. Not only that, but it is absolutely central to the church. When it is characterized again in 6:4, we find them resolving, "We will give our attention to prayer and the ministry of the Word." They would be, literally, *deacons of the Word.* This fits with what we see later in Acts 15, and again in Acts 20, and in the qualification that elders must be able to teach. It seems that the role of the elders is fundamentally to lead God's people by teaching God's Word. This teaching must be by the public handling of God's Word and also by the exemplary lives they lead.

To sum up this point, the elder's authority is directly related to his task of teaching. He is to be a pastor/shepherd. We who are elders are to serve as overseers. In Acts 6 we see the elders proposing something to the assembly. Paul in I Timothy 5 refers to the elders as "directing the affairs of the church" and "preaching and teaching." But chiefly, it seems that the elder's role is one of leading by patiently and carefully teaching.

Teaching and Authority

It would be to the great benefit of many churches to again distinguish the role of elder from that of deacon.

VI. Relationship of the Elders and "The" Pastor

If you ask the question, "Does the Bible teach that there is to be a Senior Pastor-figure alongside, or inside the eldership?" I think the answer to that question is "No, not directly." Having said that, I do think that we *can* discern a distinct role among the elders for the one who is the primary public teacher of the church.

"Pastor" only appears in the New International Version of the New Testament in Ephesians 4:11 in the list of God's gifts to his church (paired with teachers). Behind the English word "pastor" is the Greek word *poimenas* which is related to "shepherd." The related

"Pastor" in the New Testament

word for shepherd appears a few times (e.g., I Peter 5:2, Acts 20:28), but in none of these examples does a separate position from elder seem to be indicated. Indeed in Acts 20:17, 28 it is clear that "elder," "overseer [Bishop]," and "shepherd [pastor]" are all used interchangeably of the same group of people.

Glimpses of the Pastoral Role

That said, let me give you four glimpses of this kind of role that I think we see in the New Testament.

1) Even in the New Testament, there were some men who moved from place to place (like Timothy or Titus) who served as elders, and some who didn't (presumably like those that Titus [in Titus 1:5] appointed in every town). So, while Timothy came from outside, others were appointed from within the local congregation.

2) There were some who were supported full-time by the flock (cf. I Tim. 5:17-18; Philippians 4:15-18), and others who worked at another job (as Paul often did when he was first establishing the gospel in an area). One would think that not all the elders Titus made sure were appointed on Crete would have been paid full time.

3) It is interesting to note that Paul wrote to Timothy alone with instructions for the church there, even though we know from Acts that there were other elders in the Ephesian church. Timothy, though, seems in some sense to have had a unique fuction among them.

4) Finally, the letters of Jesus to the seven churches in Revelation 2 and 3 are addressed to the messenger (singular) of each of these churches.

None of these, of course, are air-tight commands, but they are descriptions that are consistent with our practice of setting aside at least one (perhaps more) from among the elders who is not necessarily from our own community, supporting that one, and giving him the primary teaching responsibility in the church.

We must, however, remember that the preacher, or pastor, is also fundamentally one of the elders of his congregation. Probably the single most helpful thing to my pastoral ministry among my church has been the recognition of the other elders. The service of the other elders along with me has had immense benefits. A plurality of elders should aid a church by rounding out the pastor's gifts, making up for some of his defects, supplementing his judgment, and creating support in the congregation for decisions, leaving leaders less exposed to unjust criticism. Such a plurality also makes leadership more rooted and permanent, and allows for more mature continuity. It encourages the church to take more responsibility for the spiritual growth of its own members and helps make the church less dependent on its employees. Our own church in Washington has enjoyed these benefits and more because of God's gift to us of elders.

The Pastor as Elder

VII. Relationship of the Elders and the Church

We'll deal with this more specifically later when we consider what we mean by congregationalism, but in general, the relationship between the elders and the local congregation they serve should be marked by many evidences of godly character and mutual dependence on God. Let me mention five characteristics of this relationship—recognition, trust, godliness, carefulness and results.

Five Characteristics of the Relationship

  1) **Clear Recognition.** Elders are to be recognized by the church as gifts from God for the good of the church. The church should therefore delegate to them the duties of teaching and leading the church. Those duties are only to be revoked when it is clear that the elders are acting in a way that is contrary to the Scriptures. And for their part, the

elders must recognize the God-given authority of the congregation (e.g., Matthew 18; I Cor. 5; II Cor. 2)

2) **Heart-felt Trust.** The church should trust, protect, respect and honor its elders. Thus Paul writes in 1 Timothy 5:17, "The elders who direct the affairs of the church well are worthy of double honor, especially those whose work is preaching and teaching." The elders should direct the affairs of the church, and the church should submit to their leadership. So the writer to the Hebrews wrote in 13:17, "Obey your leaders and submit to their authority. They keep watch over you as men who must give an account. Obey them so that their work will be a joy, not a burden, for that would be of no advantage to you."

3) **Evident Godliness.** We have seen the emphasis in Paul's letters to Timothy and Titus on the elders being "blameless." (In Titus 1:6 Paul wrote, "An elder must be blameless, the husband of but one wife, a man whose children believe and are not open to the charge of being wild and disobedient.") The elder, then, must be willing to have a life that is open to inspection and even a home that is actively open to outsiders, giving hospitality and enfolding others into their lives.

4) **Sincere Carefulness.** The elders should be marked by a use of their authority which shows that they understand that the church belongs not to them, but to Christ. Christ has purchased the church with His own blood, and therefore it should be cherished, treated carefully and gently, led faithfully and purely, for the glory of God in the good of the church. The elders will give an account to Christ for their stewardship.

5) **Beneficial Results.** As in a home, or in our own relationship with God, a humble recognition of

rightful authority brings benefits. In a church, when authority is used with the consent of the congregation for the good of the congregation, the congregation will benefitas God builds His church through the teachers He gives to His church. Satan's lie—that authority is never to be trusted because it is always tyrannical and oppressive—will be subverted by the benevolent practice of and recognition of the elders' authority in the context of the congregation.

When Edward Griffin (1770-1837) was retiring from the church he had served so well for many years, he exhorted the congregation with some words that instruct us well on how to regard not just the pastor (as Griffin then intended) but in fact all of those whom God has given us as elders:

Regard for Pastors

> For your own sake, and your children's sake, cherish and revere him whom you have chosen to be your pastor. Already he loves you; and he will soon love you as 'bone of his bone, and flesh of his flesh.' It will be equally your duty and your interest to make his labors as pleasant to him as possible. Do not demand too much. Do not require visits too frequent. Should he spend, in this way, half of the time which some demand, he must wholly neglect his studies, if not sink early under the burden. Do not report to him all the unkind things which may be said against him; nor frequently, in his presence, allude to opposition, if opposition should arise. Though he is a minister of Christ, consider that he has the feelings of a man" (Edward Griffin, *"A Tearful Farewell from a Faithful Pastor"* [1809]).

VIII. On the Gift of Authority

I hope that you see in all this that it is a great privilege to serve in leadership, one that should not be missed.

Some people may feel too busy, or think that such work is just not worth it. I'm reminded of the actor Gary Cooper's statement: "I'm just glad it'll be Clark Gable who's falling on his face and not Gary Cooper." That's what Cooper is reported to have said on rejecting the leading role in "Gone With The Wind." What we've been thinking about is so much more important than anything that would bring worldly fame or wealth. Paul says that being an elder is a "noble task" and that he who desires it desires a good thing!

One of the times that I have been most chilled in a conversation was when I was talking with someone who taught at Cambridge University. We were out at a meal, and he was expressing his anger over a recent decision of the city council. As he went on and on, I recalled how typical this was of my friend to show such anger about authority. And so at one point I asked him a simple, direct, unqualified question: "Do you think authority is bad?" Normally, such a question would earn only a puzzled look, a condescending sniffle that one would ask such a naïve question, and a meandering answer shackled by a thousand qualifications. This time, though, I was shocked by his un-nuanced, simple, direct, unqualified answer—"Yes."

A recognition of the fallen nature of authority and the possibility of its abuse is good and healthy. Power apart from God's purposes is always demonic. But a suspicion of all authority or an innate distrust of it is very bad. Really, it reveals more of the person questioning than of the authority. Moreover, it shows a cancerous degeneration in our capacity to operate as those made in God's image. To live as He meant us to live, we have to be able to trust Him, and even—to no small extent—to trust those made in His image. Everyone in the Bible from Adam and Eve to the rogue rulers in the book of Revelation show their evil fundamentally by denying God's authority, and usurping it as their own.

It is a great privilege to be served by godly leaders! To have godly authority modeled and practiced for our benefit is a great gift! To reject authority, as so many in our day do, is short-sighted and self-destructive. A world without authority would be like desires with no restraints, a car with no controls, an intersection with no traffic lights, a game with no rules, a home with no parents, a world without God. It could go on for a little while, but before long it would seem pointless, then cruel, and finally tragic.

Despite our tendency to ignore it, godly and biblical leadership is crucial to the building of a church that glorifies God. Our exercise of leadership in the church relates to God's nature and character. When we exercise proper authority through the law, around the family table, in our jobs, in the scout troop, in our homes, and especially in the church, we are helping to display God's image to His creation. This is our call. This is our privilege.

CONGREGATIONALISM

I. **Congregationalism—What it Means**
   A. Mistaken Conceptions of Congregationalism
   B. Correct Conception of Congregationalism
   C. Four Areas in the New Testament where the
      Congregation has Authority
      1. Matters of Dispute between Christians
      2. Matters of Doctrine
      3. Matters of Discipline
      4. Matters of Church Membership

II. **Congregationalism—What it Doesn't Mean**
   A. Biblical Examples of Erring Congregations
   B. Historical Examples of Erring Congregations
   C. The Picture is Incomplete, but Clear

III. **Congregationalism—Why it is Important**
   A. To Maintain Doctrinal Fidelity in
      Congregations
   B. Congregationalism's Historical Record

IV. **Congregationalism—How it Works**
   A. The Account a Leader must give
   B. Trusting Leaders
      1. Matters clear, but not serious
      2. Matters neither serious nor clear
      3. Matters both serious and clear
      4. Matters serious, but not clear
   C. Encourage and Trust your Leaders!

Chapter III

CONGREGATIONALISM

Do you consider church to exist merely for your own spiritual growth? When you gather on Sunday morning with your congregational family, you are not simply having your personal devotionals with lots of other people. No, you are participating in the life of a particular church. And when Christians gather as a congregation, it is not merely as individual consumers who happen, by temporarily shared tastes, to be in the same room. We are actually assembling as a living institution, a viable organism, one body. I wonder why YOU go to church.

Let me ask you a question that might help to get to the nub of the matter: What's the use of the church? Take a moment and try to answer that question. When you understand something more of the church and what it's about, then the Christian life becomes a lot more than a simple sustained moral effort to cultivate a list of private virtues and avoid a list of private vices. You begin to understand the church as the manifestation of the living God in this world.

I. Congregationalism—What it Means

People have often misunderstood congregationalism. Its detractors have presented it as a kind of lone-rangerish independency. "Separatism," it's been called. One writer has defined it as "the claim of individual congregations to act as if they were alone in the

Mistaken conceptions of Congregationalism

world, independently of all other Christians," (Roland Allen, *Missionary Methods*, p. 85n1). On the other hand, some of its champions have presented it as straight and simple democracy, tying it up with the inalienable rights of man. Charles Finney presented congregationalism this way:

> Episcopacy is well-suited to a state of general ignorance among the people. Presbyterianism, or Church Republicanism is better suited to a more advanced state of intelligence and the prevalence of Christian principle. While Congregationalism, or spiritual Democracy, is best suited and only suited to a state of general intelligence, and the prevalence of Christian principle. (Charles Finney in his *Lectures on Theology*)

Correct Conception of Congregationalism

None of these are good understandings of the picture of church life that the New Testament leaves us. Congregationalism in no way inhibits cooperation with other congregations in missions, education, evangelism, disaster relief, and so many other things. It does mean, though, that no body from outside can mandate something for a particular congregation, whether in a matter of discipline or of doctrine. Relying on the clarity of Scripture perhaps more than in any other polity, we congregationalists assume that God will lead His people as a whole to understand who should be recognized as members and leaders, what should be believed, and in what should be done.

Some may dismiss congregationalism as just a reflection of enlightenment political theory. But that is simply not the case. In Clement of Rome's first letter to the church at Corinth, written around AD96, we read of elders being commissioned "with the full consent of the church" *(trans. Staniforth, p. 46)*. Other examples abound. Certainly Christians in the past have understood this to be taught by Scripture.

Congregationalism is simply the understanding that the last and final court of appeal in a matter of the life of the local church is not the bishop of Rome or Constantinople or Washington. It is not some international body, or some national Assembly, Conference or Convention. It is not the president of a denomination or the chairman of a board of trustees. It is not a regional synod or ministerial association. It is not a group of elders inside the local church, or the pastor. The last and final court of appeal in a matter of the life of the local church is, and should be, the local congregation itself. This seems to be evidenced by the New Testament in matters of doctrine and of discipline, in matters of admission of members and the settling of differences between them.

Let's look at just these four matters in the New Testament:

1. Matters of Dispute between Christians. In Matthew 18:15-17, Jesus told of a dispute between brothers:

> If your brother sins against you, go and show him his fault, just between the two of you. If he listens to you, you have won your brother over. But if he will not listen, take one or two others along, so that 'every matter may be established by the testimony of two or three witnesses.' If he refuses to listen to them, tell it to the church; and if he refuses to listen even to the church, treat him as you would a pagan or a tax collector.

Notice here to whom one finally appeals. Notice what court is the final judicatory. It is not a bishop, or a presbytery; it's not an assembly, a synod, a convention or a conference. It's not a pastor or a board of elders, or a church committee. It is, we read, "the church," that is, the whole local congregation whose action must be the final court of appeal.

Four Areas in the New Testament where the Congregation has Authority.

If you look to the passage we considered earlier, Acts 6:1-5, we see an important event in the life of the early church. There was a problem over the distribution of the church's resources, and this problem was evidently requiring a good bit of the apostles' attention. Verse 2 reads,

> So the Twelve gathered all the disciples together and said, 'It would not be right for us to neglect the ministry of the Word of God in order to wait on tables. Brothers, choose seven men from among you who are known to be full of the Spirit and wisdom. We will turn this responsibility over to them and will give our attention to prayer and the ministry of the Word. This proposal pleased the whole group.

And then Luke goes on to name those whom the church chose.

One of the complexities of using the New Testament as a guide to our church life is the presence of the apostles in these churches. You understand the difficulty. How fully can we later elders, pastors and overseers assume the apostles' practice as a guide for our own? Can *we* define doctrine, delineate error, or recall the words of Christ as these could who were with Jesus throughout His earthly ministry, who were taught by Him and who were specially commissioned by Him to be the foundation of His church? Are the names of those of us who are elders here to be inscribed on the foundations of the New Jerusalem as the apostles' names are? Clearly, the answer to all these questions is "no."

Our problem with the model of the apostles is that in following it, present-day church leaders might ascribe too much authority to themselves without the competence to deserve such authority. Yet in Acts 6, we see these very apostles handing over responsibility to the congregation. They were recognizing in the assembly the same kind of ultimate authority, under God, that Jesus spoke of in Matthew 18.

Following these examples, Paul, too, taught that the discipline and doctrine of a local church is held in trust, under God, by the congregation. Paul, when writing to the Corinthian church, told them that they were to judge those inside the church (I Cor. 5:12). He writes, "appoint as judges even men of little account in the church!" (I Cor. 6:4). In matters of dispute between Christians, the congregation as a whole is the final court held out in Scripture.

2. Matters of Doctrine. All of the letters of the New Testament (except Philemon and the pastorals) were written to churches as a whole, instructing them as a whole on what their responsibilities were. Even in matters of the fundamental definition of the gospel, the congregation seemed to be the court of [earthly] final appeal. So in Galatians 1, Paul calls on congregations of fairly young Christians to sit in judgment of angelic and apostolic preachers (even himself! Gal. 1:8) if they should preach any other gospel than the one which the Galatians had accepted. He doesn't write merely to the pastors, to the presbytery, to the bishop or the conference, to the convention, or to the seminary. He writes to the Christians who compose the churches, and he makes it quite clear that not only are they competent to sit in judgement on what claims to be the gospel, but that they *must!* They have an inescapable duty to judge those who claim to be messengers of the Good News of Jesus Christ according to the consistency of their new claims with what these Galatian Christians already knew to be the gospel.

Paul makes this point again in II Timothy 4:3 when he counsels Timothy and the church in Ephesus on the best way to handle false teachers. When he describes the coming tide of false teachers in the church, he particularly blames, in 4:3, those who "to suit their own desires... gather around them a great number of teachers to say what their itching ears want to hear." Whether in selecting them, or paying for them, or approving of their teaching, or in simply consenting to listen to them repeatedly, the congregation here is culpable. They are held guilty for tolerating false teaching, as are the false teachers themselves. In basic doctrinal definition, the congregation as a whole is the final court held out in Scripture.

3. Matters of Discipline. In I Corinthians 5, Paul appeals to the whole Corinthian congregation (not just to the elders) to act, in verses 5, 7, 11, and 13. This is not a matter merely or finally for Paul the apostle, or for whatever elders the local Corinthian church may have had. This was a matter for the congregation as a whole. They had all accepted this one in to their number, and they were all now tolerating him. So they were all now implicated in his sin, and they must now either turn loose of this man, or turn loose of their claim to be Christ's disciples. In matters of church discipline, the congregation as a whole is the final court held out in Scripture.

4. Matters of Church Membership. Paul writes in II Corinthians 2:6-8, "The punishment inflicted on him by the majority is sufficient for him. Now instead, you ought to forgive and comfort him, so that he will not be overwhelmed by excessive sorrow. I urge you, therefore, to reaffirm your love for him." They had acted to punish this man. In so acting, they had done so by the majority. A majority of church members had voted to exclude this one from their fellowship. The punishment seemed to have worked. It was, as Paul says here, "sufficient for him." Now Paul writes to the church as a whole urging the repentant man's re-admission into the church. But Paul can do no more than exhort, because in matters of church membership, the congregation as a whole must be the final court. So it is in Scripture.

II. Congregationalism—What it Doesn't Mean

Saying that Scripture presents the congregation as the final court of appeal, the final earthly authority for the meaning and application of God's Word in our lives, does not mean that the congregation is always right. When Paul wrote to Timothy, his disciple and the pastor of the church in Ephesus, he described the coming evil days in II Timothy 4:3 as a time "when men will not put up with sound doctrine. Instead, to suit their own desires, they will gather around them a great number of teachers to say what their itching ears want to hear." Interesting, isn't it, that while Paul suggests that the congregation is responsible along with the elders for keeping watch over the church's doctrine (as was implied by his letter to the Galatians), he is also clear here that they will exercise that responsibility badly! Congregationalism is biblical, but the congregation is not inerrant.

Biblical Examples of Erring Congregations

This is clear from this example in II Timothy 4. It is painfully clear from the history of the church, the centuries spent largely in darkness, and even by continuing error in the congregations of brothers and sisters in whom we recognize much Biblical wisdom. Individual examples of erroneous congregational judgement abound! In history, we can go to the congregation that fired Jonathan Edwards. They had every biblical right to have that kind of authority, but that was, I think you would agree, a very poor use of it. Think, too, of our own congregations. We bring no more doubts against God's sovereignty by speaking of His churches' errors, than we do by confessing our own sins. Even rightful authority established by God in this fallen world will err.

Historical Examples of Erring Congregations

The portrayal of congregationalism in the New Testament is quite an incomplete picture. We get it in snatches, asides, and assumptions. It is, however, clearly present, and the more one thinks of it, the more

The Picture is Incomplete, but Clear

obvious it becomes throughout. Nevertheless, the peripheral, assumed nature of it would seem to leave us quite a bit of freedom to exercise the "Christian prudence, according to the general rules of the Word," of which the Westminster divines wrote (chapter one).

Almost every gathering of believers is congregational to some degree, whatever the formal structure of government. Even a church in which the congregation only holds title to the property is in some sense a congregationally governed church. In that case, the congregation could always decide simply to pull the plug on the whole thing if they didn't agree with their leaders' decisions. Even more is a church considered congregational if the congregation has the final say in issues of budget or the call of a pastor. Add to that the congregation as the final court of appeal in terms of doctrine and discipline, disputes and membership, and you begin to have a congregational church not unlike the models given us in the New Testament. How much further a congregation decides to involve itself corporately in decisions about the leadership, the staff, and the budget, is then a matter of prudence and discretion for decision within individual congregations. Neither nominating committees nor trustees are found on the pages of the New Testament. You look in vain for finance committees or small group leadership teams. Belief in the sufficiency of Scripture, however, doesn't forbid such structures; it just relativizes their authority. It clearly demonstrates that they are not of the essence of the church, and that they must submit themselves to the wisdom of the whole congregation.

III. Congregationalism—Why it is Important

Why does all this matter? If congregationalism is simply the reality of our lives together as Christians in churches, the challenge for us is not to create it, but to recognize it, and to order our church lives appropriately. We should respect the structures that God has created and trust His wisdom in doing so.

I know that some in the Reformed camp tend to lean more toward Presbyterian government. This is sometimes done quite subtly, and only half-way. For example, I know that there are many godly, congregational, baptist churches which, in deciding to have elders, decide also to have different, more stringent standards of subscription for elders than for other members of the church. For instance, they have all the members of the church affirm the New Hampshire Confession, while asking the elders to affirm the Philadelphia (or Second London) Confession in addition. While the desire for exemplary maturity in the elders of a congregation is healthy and even biblical, this means of achieving it may leave something to be desired. Do we see such clearly modeled in Scripture? No. Would this perhaps leave the congregation both feeling and appearing unprepared to be the court of final appeal in matters of doctrine, as Paul commanded them to be in Galatians? You must decide for yourself. While I will certainly desire and probably expect a more mature understanding of doctrine from those who would serve us as elders, I would not want to move the church to a more clergy-dependent position than I find on the pages of the New Testament; I fear that such formal requirements may tend to that.

To Maintain Doctrinal Fidelity in Congregations

Friends, the verdict of history is in. While it is clear that no certain polity prevents churches from error, from declension, and from sterility, the more centralized polities seem to have a worse track record than does congregationalism in maintaining a faithful, vital, evangelical witness. (Congregationalism's record is particularly enhanced in the case when the purity and visibility of the church is protected through a biblical practice of believer baptism and a rejection of infant baptism.) The papacy has wrought havoc on

Congregationalism's Historical Record

self-confessed Christians. Bishops have hardly done better. Even assemblies, conferences, presbyteries, synods and sessions, when they have moved from being advisors to being rulers, have overstepped their scripturally-warranted authority and have brought more trouble than help.

Could it be that the gospel itself is so simple and clear, and the relationship that we have with God by the Holy Spirit's action in giving us the new birth is so real that the collection of those who believe the gospel and who know God are simply the best guardians of that gospel? Doesn't that seem to be what we see in the Scriptures?

IV. Congregationalism—How it Works

The Account a Leader Must Give

As congregationalists, how should we respond to Hebrews 13:17? "Obey your leaders and submit to their authority. They keep watch over you as men who must give an account. Obey them so that their work will be a joy, not a burden, for that would be of no advantage to you." This didn't mean, of course, that the writer was telling these Christians to become the menial hand-waiters to their leaders. No, the seriousness of the topic in mind is clear. This has to do with the account these leaders will give for their work, and that account is given to God!

Does this have any wider implications? I think so, in that it is always helpful for Christians to have in mind the seriousness of positions of authority in the church, particularly in matters of teaching. James said in James 3:1 that "Teachers will be judged with a stricter judgment." The account that we elders must give is finally not to our churches; it is to God.

Trusting Leaders

Do you see the importance of all this? In all the corporate responsibility we have, I am not suggesting that God leaves us merely to operate all the time as a committee of the whole. We should give thanks to God for the leaders that He puts among us. We should recognize them, and trust them. The words we see here like "obey" and "submit" are words that we are not used to hearing, but they are words that are applied in the New Testament to people in society and at work, at home and in our marriages, with God and in the church. And they do require, on our part, a certain amount of trust.

It has been said that trust must be earned. I understand what is meant. When a new administration comes in, a new boss is put in place at work, or even a new friendship starts, we want to see by experience how these people will weather the difficulties, how they persevere, whether they succeed in benefiting not just themselves, but others, too. So, we say, trust is earned.

But that attitude is at best only half true. At the same time, the kind of trust that we are called to give to our fellow imperfect humans in this life, be they family or friends, employers or government officials, or even leaders in our church, can never finally be earned. It

	↑
Clear, but not Serious	Both Serious & Clear
Neither Serious nor Clear	Serious but not Clear

Increasing Clarity

Increasing Seriousness ⟹

must be given as a gift—a gift in faith, more in trust of the God who gives, than of those whom we see as God's gifts to us. It is a serious spiritual deficiency in a church either to have leaders who are untrustworthy or members who are incapable of trusting.

So how should we trust? Imagine a simple graph, with one line measuring increasing clarity and another increasing seriousness. The quadrants are 1) those things which are clear, but not serious, 2) those things which are neither serious nor clear, 3) those things which are both serious and clear, and 4) those things which are certainly serious, but are not clear.

1. Clear, but not Serious (e.g., Should we paint the exterior of the building purple?)—On matters in this category, there will simply be no discussion generally, though under "Any Other Business" I'm never sure what's going to come up!

2. Neither Serious nor Clear (e.g., Should we close our services with prayer or with a time of silence?)—On these matters, good and spirited congregational discussion is fine. These are not entirely unimportant matters, but neither are they the most important. Everything from cleaning contracts to parking ideas could be included here.

3. Both Serious and Clear (e.g., Should we continue to require belief that Jesus is fully God and fully man in order to be a member of our church?)—There will almost always be agreement here, but should there be serious errors by the elders in either doctrine or discipline, this is where the apostles always appeal to the congregation in the New Testament. Would the church at Jerusalem split? Would the church at Corinth forfeit their witness to God's holiness, and lead people astray about what it meant to be a Christian? Would the church at Corinth refuse to recognize genuine repentance? Would the churches of Galatia forfeit the Gospel? Would the church at Ephesus accept false teaching? In these clearest matters of congregational action in the New Testament, the greatest of issues are at stake.

4. Serious, but not Clear (e.g., Should we acknowledge this person as an elder or affirm this membership action; should we allocate this serious expenditure, or make this directional decision as a congregation?)— These are the issues about which it is most important for the church to listen to the elders. In many ways, it is this quadrant where the elders most particularly serve the church, rather than the church attempting to act as a committee of the whole, or the pastor, or some committee chairman, making the decision alone. This is the crucial area where a church either enjoys the leadership God gives it and prospers by it, or they reject it and pay the price.

A church member's basic attitude needs to be either to trust the leaders or replace them. But don't say that you acknowledge them and then not follow them. If you disagree with the elders on a recommendation, have a good reason. Go and talk with them about it. Other than the Bible, you are the elders' main source of information about YOU! Rather than distrusting church leaders, let me encourage you to talk behind your elders' backs, meet in secret and plot to encourage your leaders. Strategize to make the church leaders' work not burdensome, but a joy. This, the writer to the Hebrews says, will make your leaders a blessing to you.

Encourage and Trust your Leaders!

John Brown, a teacher of ministers in Scotland two hundred years ago, wrote a letter of paternal counsels to one of his pupils newly ordained over a small congregation. In it he said,

> I know the vanity of your heart, and that you will feel mortified that your congregation is very small, in comparison with those of your brethren around

you; but assure yourself on the word of an old man, that when you come to give an account of them to the Lord Christ, at his judgment-seat, you will think you have had enough.

How many churches languish today in an evil combination of selfish leaders and stubborn members? Such congregations usually shrink and wither away. Some churches have wonderful congregations, but they have recognized the wrong people as pastors and elders, people who show themselves to be at best careless, and at worst, base charlatans. Too many of us have been involved in such churches. Some churches have wonderful, godly leaders, but congregations full of complacent, self-centered people. If such a pastor can stay and patiently teach, the congregation can be renewed. If not, such a congregation will, I think, bear a heavy judgement on the final day for wounding good under-shepherds of the flock of Christ. But the healthy church, though filled with imperfect members and leaders, is marked by godly initiative and service, godly teaching and obedience, godly leadership and membership.

It is to that broader idea of membership that we now turn.

MEMBERSHIP

I.   **Commitment-phobia and Membership**

II. **What is a Church?**
  A. The "church" is not a Building
  B. The Church is a Clearly Defined, Distinct Community
    1. In the New Testament
    2. In the Old Testament
    3. Baptists are historically unique in this understanding
    4. A side note to historians

III. **Why Join a Church?**
  A. Importance of the Question
  B. Five Reasons to Join a Church
    1. To Assure Ourselves
    2. To Evangelize the World
    3. To Expose False Gospels
    4. To Edify the Church
    5. To Glorify God

IV. **Marks of Church Membership**
  A. Baptism
    1. Evidence against Infant Baptism
    2. Biblical Evidence for Believer Baptism
  B. The Lord's Supper
  C. Attendance
  D. Discipline
  E. Love

Chapter IV

MEMBERSHIP

Let's begin by admitting that the whole idea of church membership seems counter-productive to many today. Isn't it unfriendly, and maybe even elitist, to say that some are in and others out? Can we go so far as to say that it is even unbiblical, and maybe even unChristian? The end of Acts 2 simply says that "the Lord added to their number" (that is, to the church) those who were being saved. Isn't that all there is to it? In Acts 8, an official of the Ethiopian government had been traveling in Palestine and was returning home on his chariot, reading the prophet Isaiah. Philip was led by the Holy Spirit to intercept him and talk to him; the man believed and was baptized. In that case, wasn't the Ethiopian automatically a member of the church?

I. Commitment-phobia and membership

All of this is more important than many people today think it is. In fact, I'm convinced that getting this right is a key step toward revitalizing our churches, evangelizing our nation, furthering the cause of Christ around the world, and so bringing glory to God!

American evangelicals are in pretty desperate need of rethinking and reconsidering this topic, especially our own fellowship of churches in the Southern Baptist Convention. According to one Southern Baptist study a few years ago, the typical Southern Baptist church has 233 members with 70 present at the

Sunday morning worship service. My question is this: where are the other 163 members? Are they all at home sick, in a rest home, at college, on vacation, or in the military? Maybe some are, but all 163 of them? What does this convey about Christianity to the world around us? What do we understand this to mean about the importance of Christianity in our lives? And what is the spiritual state of those people, if they've not been at church for months, or even longer? Is their non-attendance really any of our business? To understand this, we need to first ask the question, "What is a church?"

II. What is a Church?

By the word "church" we refer not to an organizational unit of a religion. We don't refer to Buddhist churches or Jewish churches. By "church," we don't fundamentally mean a building; only in a secondary sense is it that. The building is simply where the church meets, thus the New England puritan name for the church building, "meeting house." The earliest New England churches looked like large houses from the outside. It was just the house where the church met.

According to the New Testament, the church is primarily a regular assembly of people who profess and give evidence that they have been saved by God's grace alone through faith alone in Christ alone to the glory of God alone. This is what a New Testament church is; it is not a building. The early Christians didn't have any buildings for almost three hundred years after the church began. From the earliest of times, though, local Christian churches were clearly congregations of specific people. Certain people would have been known to make up this assembly, and others clearly known as outside of it. Thus the censures taught by Jesus in Matthew 18 and Paul in I Corinthians 5 envision an

The "Church" is Not a Building

The Church is a Clearly Defined Community

In the New Testament

individual being excluded, not from a political community, but from a distinct social one. While we don't know for sure that physical lists of members existed in the earliest Christian churches, they may have. The idea was not unheard-of. We know that the early church kept lists of widows; we know that God Himself is presented as having a list of those in the universal church in the Book of Life. And we know from II Corinthians 2 that both Paul and the Corinthians could clearly identify a majority of a certain set of people which they understood to be those who were members of the church, i.e. those who were eligible to vote.

The idea of a clearly defined community of people is central to God's action in both the Old and the New Testaments. From God working with Noah and his family, to Abraham and his descendants, to the nation of Israel, to the church in the New Testament, God has chosen to maintain a distinct and clearly separate people in order to display His character. God's intention has always been that there be a sharp, bright line distinguishing those who trust in Him from those who do not.

In the Old Testament

This concept of the church as a gathered community is something that has distinguished Baptist Christians from many others. At the time of the Reformation the relationship between state and church was both close and complicated. The discipline of either the church or the state often carried consequences from the other as well. It was assumed that everyone born within the bounds of a certain political jurisdiction should be able to be a member of the state church. The recovery of the baptism of believers at the time of the Reformation threatened this association at its very roots as Baptists recovered the New Testament idea of the church as a congregation of those both personally professing and giving evidence of regeneration.

Baptist are Historically Unique in this Understanding

One interesting side note for historians—the church as a voluntarily covenanted community of believers is an important contribution that Baptists particularly have made to our nation's religious liberty. This may surprise you. Some today see Baptists as the forces of benighted, oppressive, religious totalitarianism. But that is far from the case historically, and it is terribly ironic. In some senses, the freedom some use to speak and write about our bigotry is protected by the very understanding of the church that we Christians who are Baptists have advocated in this country for three centuries.

The church is not finally something that is for you and every member of your family by physical, natural descent, or by virtue of your citizenship in this nation. No, the New Testament teaches that the church is for believers. So we advocate laws in this land that provide the kind of freedom for that church to be able to operate in liberty. Baptists are not, then, advocating a new established church in America; indeed we are its firmest foes. Our very understanding of the church will not allow that. We are advocating the evangelization of the nation through churches that freely cooperate together in the gospel of Jesus Christ. And a church is a local collection of Christians committed to Christ and to each other.

III. Why Join a Church?

This topic is a must for our churches, and for us as individual Christians today. It is a crucial topic for understanding what Christ is calling you to as a disciple of Him. Joining a church will not save you any more than your good works, your education, your culture, your friendships, your contributions, or your baptism will save you. Non-Christians shouldn't be trying to join a church, but to learn more what it means to be a Christian. But for those who are confessing Christians, let me ask the question: What does it mean to live the Christian life? Do we live the Christian life alone?

There are many other good questions we could ask which would point up our need for a church, but let me give you five good reasons to join a church which preaches the gospel, and models Christian living.

Five Reasons to Join a Church

1. To Assure Ourselves — You should not join the church in order to be saved, but you should join the church to help you in making certain that you are saved. Remember the words of Jesus in John's gospel?

> "Whoever has my commands and obeys them, he is the one who loves me. He who loves me will be loved by my Father, and I too will love him and show myself to him.... If you obey my commands, you will remain in my love, just as I have obeyed my Father's commands and remain in His love.... You are my friends if you do what I command.... Now that you know these things, you will be blessed if you do them" (John 14:21; 15:10, 14; 13:17).

In joining the church, we put ourselves in a position where we ask our brothers and sisters to hold us accountable to live according to what we speak with our mouth. We ask them to encourage us sometimes by reminding us of ways that they have seen God work in our lives, and other times to challenge us when we may be moving away from obedience to Him. Your membership in a local church is that congregation's public testimony that your life gives evidence of regeneration.

Membership in a local church is not saving, but it is a reflection of salvation. And if there is no reflection, how are we to know about the salvation claimed?

In becoming a member of the church, we are grasping hands with each other to know and be known by each other, and to help and encourage one another when we may need to be reminded of God's work in our lives, or to be challenged about major discrepancies between our talk and our walk.

2. To Evangelize the World — You should join a local church also for the sake of evangelizing the world. Together we can better spread the gospel at home and abroad. We can do this by our words, as we share the message of the good news with others, and as we help others to do that. A local church is, by nature, a missionary organization.

We back this up with our actions as we work to show God's love by meeting the physical needs of orphans, the sick, children, or the disadvantaged. Through our own fellowship of churches we help spread the gospel around the world, and we provide millions of dollars and thousands of volunteers to help those who have some immediate physical needs like disaster relief, education, and countless other ministries. Even as imperfect as we are, if God's spirit is genuinely at work in us, He will use our lives and words to help demonstrate to others the truth of His gospel. This is a special role now that we won't have in Heaven. This is the special privilege of the church now—to be part of God's plan, to take His gospel to the world.

3. To Expose False Gospels — God intends us to be together in this way to expose false gospels. It is through our coming together as Christians that we show the world what Christianity really is. In our churches, we debunk messages and images which purport to be biblical Christianity but really are not. Must it not surely be the case that some of those who are not members of evangelical churches are not so because they do not really believe the same evangel? Part of the church's mission is to recognize and defend the true gospel and to prevent perversions of it. We must realize that part of our task in evangelizing may very well be not only to present positively the gospel of Jesus Christ, but also to dismantle the bad, confusing, distorted witnesses that have raised themselves up as Christian churches, yet which in reality confuse the gospel more than they confirm it.

4. To Edify the Church — A fourth reason for joining the church is the edification or building up of the church. Joining a church will help counter our wrong individualism and will help us to realize the corporate nature of Christianity. When you study the New Testament you find that our Christian lives are supposed to involve our care and concern for each other. That is part of what it means to be a Christian. And though we do it imperfectly, we should be committed to do this. We intend to encourage even baby steps in righteousness, love, selflessness and Christlikeness.

In our church's membership class I often tell the story of a friend who worked for a campus Christian ministry while attending a church in which I was a member. He would always slip in right after the hymns, sit there for the sermon, and then leave. I asked him one day, why he didn't come for the whole service. "Well," he said, "I don't get anything out of the rest of it." "Have you ever thought about joining the church?" I responded. He thought that was just an absurd question. He said, "Why would I join the church? If I join them, I think they would just slow me down spiritually." When he said this I wondered what he understood being a Christian to mean. I replied, "Have you ever considered that maybe God wants you to link arms with those other people? Sure, they might slow you down, but you might help to speed them up. Maybe that's part of God's plan for us as we live together as Christians!"

5. To Glorify God — Finally, a Christian should join a church for the glory of God. Peter wrote to some early Christians, "Live such good lives among the pagans that, though they accuse you of doing wrong, they may see your good deeds and glorify God on the day he visits us" (I Peter 2:12). Amazing, isn't it? But then again, you can tell that Peter had heard the teaching of His Master. You remember what Jesus had taught in the Sermon on the Mount. "Let your light shine before men, that they may see your good deeds and praise your Father in heaven" (Matthew 5:16). Again, the surprising assumption seems to be that God will receive the glory for our good works. If that is true of our lives individually, it shouldn't come as too much of a surprise to find that God's Word says that this is also the case with our lives together as Christians. God intends that the way we love each other will identify us as followers of Christ. Recall Jesus' famous words in John 13:34-35, "A new command I give you: Love one another. As I have loved you, so you must love one another. All men will know that you are my disciples if you love one another." Our lives together are to mark us out as His, and are to bring Him praise and glory.

IV. Marks of Church Membership

Given that we are in a fallen world, and are in at least partial league with it, how do we determine who is and who is not a member of a particular church? Who is in and who is out?

Baptism First, to be a member of a church, you should have been baptized as a believer in confession of your sins and as a profession that you have repented of them and are trusting in Christ alone for your salvation. Scripture records in Matthew 28 Jesus's clear command to baptize those who become disciples. Throughout the book of Acts, we see that the disciples understood and obeyed this command.

We believe that baptism is reserved for those who have made a conscious profession of faith in Christ. Because of this, we believe that it is an error of doctrine to practice the baptism of infants. Let me give you five reasons for this belief.

1) Nobody disagrees with believer baptism. The debated point is infant baptism.

2) There are no clear examples in the New Testament of infant baptism.

3) There is no clear teaching on infant baptism in the New Testament.

4) The New Testament nowhere teaches a parallel of physical circumcision with physical baptism. In fact, Colossians 2 exactly parallels *spiritual* circumcision with physical baptism, that is, the circumcision *of the heart* with physical baptism. This would support the idea of baptizing only those who give evidence of being born again.

5) Historically, infant baptism is not in the New Testament, and it is not in the *Didache*, an early second-century manual of Christian worship. There is no certain record of it in the first century, or even in the second century. In the third century, there is certain record of infant baptism, but it is not the infant baptism which some of our Reformed Protestant friends teach. It is rather what the Roman Catholic church now teaches— that baptism actually effects our being born again, our regeneration, our salvation. The idea of infant baptism that some of our reformed Protestant friends teach, in fact, does not appear until after other Protestants in the 1520's have re-introduced the practice of believer baptism. It is really Huldrich Zwingli who pioneers the idea of an infant baptism that is not salvific or regenerating.

Paul's assumption in his letters seems to be that those who are baptized have experienced new life (Romans 6), those who have had their hearts circumcised (Colossians 2). Baptism, then, is essential for membership in a church because if one were to be

Evidence Against Infant Baptism

Biblical Evidence for Believer Baptism

admitted by a church, only to refuse such a clear command of Christ, then such an unbaptized person claiming to follow Christ would simply be immediately disciplined until they either decided to follow Christ's commands, or stopped having the church's endorsement of their claim to follow Him. There will never be anything that Jesus calls you to do that will be easier than baptism.

The Lord's Supper

Being a member of a church should mean being present at the Lord's Supper. This means, essentially, that you are continuing on as a Christian. Scripture records Jesus' commands to His disciples to take the supper of bread and wine as He said in His own words about the bread "in remembrance of me." About the cup, He said, "do this, whenever you drink it, in remembrance of me." We know from Paul's first letter to the Corinthians that this was being done then, and it has continued to be done by confessing Christians since that time. The church's appearance at the Lord's Supper is the symbolic appearance of the church as the gathering of those who are feeding by faith on Christ.

Attendance

Being a member of a church should mean regularly being present at public meetings. Attendance is perhaps our most basic ministry to each other. As the oft-quoted Hebrews 10:25 says, "Let us not give up meeting together, as some are in the habit of doing, but let us encourage one another—and all the more as you see the Day approaching."

If the New Testament uses the image of the church as a building, then we must be bricks in it; if the church is a body, then we are its members; if the church is the household of faith, it presumes we are part of that household. Sheep are in a flock, and branches on a vine. Biblically, if one is a Christian he must be a member of a church. And this membership is not simply the record of a statement we once made or of affection toward a familiar place. It must be the reflection of a living commitment, a regular attendance, or it is worthless, and worse than worthless, it is dangerous.

Uninvolved "members" confuse both real members and non-Christians about what it means to be a Christian. And we "active" members do the voluntarily "inactive" members no service when we allow them to remain members of the church; for membership is the church's corporate endorsement of a person's salvation. We need to understand this: membership in a church is that church's corporate testimony to the individual member's salvation. Yet how can a congregation honestly testify that someone invisible to it is faithfully running the race?

In our own church, we are constantly trying to notice those who have simply slipped away from attending, and we try to either bring them back, or care for them specially (if they're in the military or in college, or unable to leave their home due to illness). If someone is able to attend a church, our intent is that they should as soon as possible be taken out of membership here, so that they are encouraged to join where they can regularly attend.

Another clear aspect of membership in a church is one I've just mentioned—discipline. From Jesus' Discipline teaching in Matthew 18 to Paul's in I Corinthians 5 and Galatians 6, it is indisputable that one of the functions of a local church family is to draw boundaries which will exclude people who are themselves unwilling to be excluded from membership in the church. For more information on this vital but neglected topic, see the work of Jay Adams, *Handbook of Church Discipline* (Zondervan, 1986) and Mark Dever ed., *Polity: Biblical Arguments on How to Conduct Church Life* (Center for Church Reform, 2001). Adams approaches the subject from a Presbyterian viewpoint, while the second book is a compilation of ten volumes from early Baptists.

Although the two books approach the topic of discipline from different church polities, there is substantial agreement between them. Both works should be useful to any pastor or church leader.

Love must be seen in those who are members of the church. In John 13 Jesus told His disciples, "A new command I give you: Love one another. As I have loved you, so you must love one another. All men will know that you are my disciples if you love one another" (John 13:35). Should someone decide that they can appropriately call themselves a Christian without being in committed loving relationships with other Christians, they should carefully consider what we read in I John 4:20, "If anyone says, 'I love God,' yet hates his brother, he is a liar. For anyone who does not love his brother, whom he has seen, cannot love God, whom he has not seen." Given our propensity to deceive ourselves, to over-estimate our own goodness, thank God that He has given us such checks on our own pride and blindness! Giving and receiving Christian love is clearly part of what the Bible teaches that it means to be a member of a church, and we do this in every way from tithing our income for the support of the ministry, to warmly greeting those whom we don't know.

Many, many other things flow out of this in a local church. For example, we ask members of our church to sign a statement of faith and a covenant—a statement of how that one will act among us. We expect that members will pray for the church, that they will give financially to support the church, and that they will be involved in ministries of the church. Baptism, the Lord's Supper, Attendance, Discipline, and Love are something of the heart of local church membership.

So, my Christian friend, do not merely attend a church (though you should attend), but join a church. Link arms with other Christians. Find a church you can join, and do it so that non-Christians will hear and see the gospel, so that weak Christians will be cared for, so that strong Christians will channel their energies in a good way, so that church leaders will be encouraged and helped, so that God will be glorified.

CONCLUSION

Paul's first letter to the Corinthians is a wonderful letter to read and meditate on if you want to understand more of what life together as a church entails. What you find there is that we as a church are to be marked especially by Holiness, Unity, and Love.

Why is the church to be like this? Because the character of the church is to reflect the character of God. We are to be holy and united and loving essentially because God is like all these things. We are to be holy because God is holy. We are to be united because God is one. We are to be loving because God is love.

First, we are to be holy in the sense of being strange to the world, but special to God. We are to be pure. Holiness is to be an attribute which marks the church. It is to be a trademark; it is to be common among us, and typical. When someone considers our particular church, they are to think, "That is a holy community."—*not* meaning a bunch of self-righteous, prudish people, but a community that in our conduct holds out hope of a better, more humane, more God-honoring way of living. That's why all these matters of membership and teaching and discipline are important. We are to be holy because God is holy.

Also, we are to be united because God is One. It's very interesting in I Corinthians chapter 1, when Paul begins with the ill report he had heard of the various divisions and factions in the church, that the apostle deals with the issue theologically. Look at the question he poses to them in light of their divisions in I Corinthians 1:13: "Is Christ divided?" What a fascinating question! When you think about it, no local church has any other basis for being. When Paul looks at the divisions in the church and then turns to ask, "Is Christ divided?" the powerful theological assumption behind it is that the church is the body of Christ. That idea reminds us of the serious responsibility we have to reflect God. Our divisions take on an added seriousness because, as with any unholiness or blame, they reflect on the One whom we are to image. Our disunity is really a lie about God and what He is like.

As Paul said in I Corinthians 12:27, "You are the body of Christ, and each one of you is a part of it." Where do you think Paul got that idea? I think he got it in the very hour he was converted. In Acts 9 when Paul is stopped in his tracks by an appearance of the Risen Christ, he was on his way to persecute the Christians in Damascus. What did Christ say to him? "Saul, Saul, why are you persecuting Christians?" No. "Saul, Saul, why are you persecuting the church?" No. He said, "Saul, Saul, why are you persecuting me?" This is how closely Jesus relates to His church. He views it as His body, and us as members of that body!

One of the main reasons that we are called in I Corinthians to "get rid" of those committed to their sins more than to Christ is because we are to be united. Unity was supposed to be one of the hallmarks of the church. This unity was to transcend the old divisions of Jew and Gentile (I Cor. 7:19), along with every other worldly division. This is why Paul was so upset by the report of divisions in the church. Even at the feast of the their unity—the Lord's Supper—they were divided. When churches divide for carnal reasons, we start being about other things—we are the church of modern music, or of this pastor, or the church of the home-schoolers, or of the Democrats, or the church of the blue carpet. All of these unities are different from true Christian unity. The church is to be united.

Finally, we are to be loving because God is loving. The only way that we can be united is in love. In I Corinthians 8:1, Paul writes that "We know that we all possess knowledge. Knowledge puffs up, but love builds up." This becomes Paul's basis for his large excursion in chapters 8-14 on letting love and consideration for others be the governor of what we should do. Paul had a love for God's church at heart. So he wrote in 14:26, "All of these must be done for the strengthening of the church." And in verse 31, "so that everyone may be instructed and challenged." Paul was quite sensitive to the church's health, wasn't he? No wonder then, when you look at 15:9 and remember his history, "For I am the least of the apostles and do not even deserve to be called an apostle, because I persecuted the church of God." Surely we can see why God would use such a man to teach us, as he says in 16:14, "Do everything in love."

Consider the love that Christ has shown by pouring out his blood and by offering up his body for us (I Cor. 11:23-26). Christians have known this from the earliest times. So we read in I Corinthians 15:3-5, a sort of early church creed. And in 15:3, "Christ died for our sins," (cf. Rom.5:6-8; Gal. 2:21; I Pet. 3:18).

One particularly interesting part of that love is the concern for other churches which they had and which Paul called for. From the very beginning of the letter, they could not help but be reminded of this: Paul writes to the Corinthians "together with all those everywhere" (I Corinthians 1:2). Paul, too, had behaved in this way toward them. So in I Corinthians 4:17, we find Paul sending his beloved Timothy to them. Then in the last chapter, in 16:1-4, Paul wrote to them "about the collection for God's people." These early Christians were, in love, trying to find ways to help others. Is our church marked by such love? The church is to be loving because God is loving.

The church is to be the display of God's love in the midst of this messed up, sinful, selfish world. Are we that? Do we as a church display the character of God?

This is the kind of exalted language we find in the New Testament about the church! We read in Ephesians 5:25 that "Christ loved the church, and gave himself up for her." Acts 20:28 teaches us that God gave Himself for His church; He bought His church with His own blood. If we are His followers, we too will love the church for which Christ gave Himself. Why does God so care for the church? Because He wants to glorify Himself through it.

One of the most intriguing statements in the New Testament to me is I Corinthians 15:19, in which Paul says, "If only for this life we have hope in Christ, we are to be pitied more than all men." This is an important statement for wrongly-satisfied Christians. Too many churches today present a version of Christianity in which all sufferings are made up for, all sacrifices rewarded, all mysteries explained, in this life. But this is not the gospel that Paul taught; in fact, this is not the gospel of our Lord Christ. And this must not be the gospel of our churches. If you evaluate a Christian's life this side of eternity, it will not add up. Christ's didn't; Paul's didn't. Ours shouldn't either.

Finally, you see, Paul did what he did for the sake of the gospel (see I Cor. 9:23). Is that why our church does what it does? If we are to be the kind of congregation that God desires, and that brings God glory, we should be a congregation that is oriented to this final hope in everything from our gospel message, to our lives of sacrificial love toward each other (see Hebrews 10:34). Only by being so will we be faithful representatives of our great God!

You see, this is what God is doing in the church! In I Corinthians 1, Paul said (1:28-29) that God "chose the lowly things of this world and the despised things— and the things that are not, so that no one may boast before him." Do you know why God chooses to use people like you and me, things as apparently weak as the church? Because He does not in any way want to obscure Himself!

At a conference I attended a couple of years ago, I heard Mark Ross of First Presbyterian Church, Columbia, South Carolina make the point that, "We are one of God's chief pieces of evidence." He continued, "Paul's great concern [in Eph. 4:1-16] for the church," he said, "is that the church manifest and display the glory of God, thus vindicating God's character against all the slander of demonic realms, the slander that God is not worth living for. God has entrusted to His church the glory of His own name. The circumstances of your life are the God-given occasion of your displaying and manifesting the attributes of God."

If we're not careful, our individualism can be used to harbor a sub-Christian holiness which tolerates sin. Our selfishness can lead us to a sub-Christian unity which papers over disunity about the gospel, and unites around other, lesser things. Even our flesh can know a sub-Christian love which is mere sentiment, having a family feeling because we've all been together so long. But friends, none of these things should characterize our church primarily because all of these things *lie about God*. They misrepresent His character. True holiness will include discipline. And true unity will be only around Christ—and the diversity of the church will give evidence to this. True love will go deeper than sentiment, beyond natural bounds. It will go out to the stranger for Christ's sake. *This* is how God's glory is displayed in the church. This is the only way a church will truly prosper.

So how do we display God's glory? By organizing our churches after the pattern He has shown us in His Word. By living for Him, with a life of holiness, unity and love. This is what the church is devoted to. Are you?

SCRIPTURE INDEX